D1097719

Japanese Gardens Today

Japanese Gardens Today

how the Japanese use rocks, water, plants

by TATSUO and KIYOKO ISHIMOTO

CROWN PUBLISHERS, INC., NEW YORK

Library of Congress Catalog Card Number: 68–9077
Printed in the United States of America
Published simultaneously in Canada by
General Publishing Company Limited

Table of Contents

Introduction

Our first book on Japanese garden design, *The Art of the Japanese Garden,* was published just ten years ago, in 1958. It was based on a photographic tour of Honshu, Japan's main island.

Now that a decade had passed, we thought, Why not go back again to have a more intensive look, to travel more extensively? Our publishers agreed, and back we went last year. This time we traveled north all the way to Hokkaido, the large northernmost island, then south to Kyushu and the southernmost tip of Japan. We traveled by air, by bus and by car, by steamer, by ferry, by train and "supertrain." But also, and mostly, we walked—for miles and miles.

Along the way we exposed 350 rolls of film—some 4,000 pictures—almost all of them in gardens; about 200 of the best of them are now in this book.

Japan includes more than 3,000 islands, but the four important islands are Hokkaido, Honshu, Shikoku, and Kyushu. You will see pictures of gardens on all these islands in this new book.

From the mail we receive and from the way our earlier book on Japanese garden design keeps selling, it is obvious that many Americans are interested in, and curious about, the Japanese approach to home landscaping. If our earlier *The Art of the Japanese Garden* was intended as a primer on Japanese landscaping, this new book is intended as an appreciation of Japanese landscaping. The two books are actually complementary. For more about the art of shaping plants in gardens, see our recent book *The Art of Shaping Shrubs, Trees, and Other Plants* (1966). If you are interested in what the Japanese garden is today, and how it evolved, this new book of ours should help you. That is its purpose. Turn the page and join us on an appreciative tour of Japan and Japanese gardens today.

TATSUO AND KIYOKO ISHIMOTO

Mount Yotei, one of most beautiful mountains in Japan, is in southwest Hokkaido. This mountain is not so tall as Fujisan (Mount Fuji) near Hakone.

Beautiful Japan

Japan is beautiful wherever you go. Surrounded by water, and with its land area for the most part mountainous, the country has great scenic variety.

Japan's generally mild climate is hospitable to plant life. Spring is a glorious time. New shoots appear; trees burst into leaf in different shades of green; and all sorts of lovely flowers bloom. It is the time of cherry blossoms and of azaleas showing white, pink, and red. In the autumn, the countryside is tinted gold to crimson as the leaves of maples and other trees change color.

Japan resembles Europe in many of its tourist features. Very popular today are aerial tramways, and some of the gondolas carry over a hundred persons. Typically, they take you from a bus terminal to an observatory, high on a mountain, that commands a panoramic view. You may then climb a zigzag road to the summit, if you wish.

Among many fascinating things we saw from a train were some three-story-high box-shaped pine hedges growing around houses to shelter them from strong sea breezes in the Izumo Plain. We were fascinated, went back, and spent an afternoon inspecting them at close range.

Another fascinating scenic attraction is the Kujukushima (Ninety-nine Islands) near the city of Sasebo.

Cape Sata, lying at the southern extremity of Kyushu, at 31° north latitude, faces the Pacific Ocean and the East China Sea. These islands are covered with tropical trees. Boats are the only means of transportation.

Nagasakibana, on the East China Sea, across the horseshoe-shaped Kagoshima Bay from Cape Sata, is also on the southern tip of Kyushu. The tall trees are pines. It is still Japan, though the mountain, the palms, the house, and the cranes create an exotic tropical atmosphere.

Actually, the group consists of over 170 pine-covered, gem-like islands of different shapes and sizes. The name Ninety-nine Islands is derived from the concept of "foreverness," which the number ninety-nine signifies in Japanese. Therefore, instead of "One Hundred" or "One Hundred and Seventy," the group of islands was named Ninety-nine, a more dramatic and celebrated name.

We saw a superb waterfall in the garden of the Sapporo Park Hotel. We watched active volcanoes in Hokkaido and Kyushu. We visited various hot-springs (*onsen*) resorts, as well as gardens, tropical jungles, villages, and the site of the Imperial Palace before the first emperor set out to rule over Japan.

Though the many gardens we saw on our trip from north to south through Japan were different in appearance, they also had a family resemblance. They were similar in inspiration, natural materials, and their use of ornamental objects. Throughout Japan, in large and bustling cities and in small hidden villages, you will find beautiful gardens. But perhaps Kyoto, the home of a traditional culture over a thousand years old, contains the most truly splendid examples of Japanese garden design.

There are acres and acres of rice fields in Aso Valley. The neatly diked paddy segments form an abstract mosaic composition.

This active volcano suddenly rose from a vegetable field near Lake Toya in 1944. The fumes are coming out of fissures in the side of the mountain. Today the volcano is a great attraction in Japan.

The dark wall is made by three-story-high hedges of pine. The trees are pruned in a square shape to act as a windbreak. The pine belts shelter the farmhouses in the rice fields from the strong sea breeze that sweeps across the Izumo Plain.

There are many famous rock and sand gardens in Japan. This is the garden of Tofukuji. The sand area is flat, but the way it is raked makes it appear to undulate. If you cover the rocks with your hand, the wavelike effect is more marked.

Great effort has gone into training these pine branches. The basic idea is similar to that of topiary and espalier work. The bamboo poles, to which the branches are tied, guide the growth, while vertical poles support the branches.

This is a large pine in a nursery yard in Takamatsu. If you wish, you can buy it, and the nursery will deliver and plant it on the site you select.

This aged bonsai is *nishiki-matsu* (Japanese black pine). This species has extraordinarily developed cork tissue around the trunk, and is native to Shikoku. Kinashi-machi, near Takamatsu, produces some of the finest bonsai in Japan.

In the lobby of the Ginza-Tokyu Hotel in Tokyo, we heard an interesting sound at regular intervals. The sound came from this unit consisting of a stone, water basin, and bamboo pipe. Japanese call this device *sozu,* of which we shall see more in later pages.

Japan, too, has its "largest" and "most famous." This is the largest stone lantern in Japan. It is in Kagoshima.

In Japan today, collecting natural stones for display has become fashionable. From Hokkaido in the north to Kyushu in the south, such stones are popular items in gift shops. This display was in the Gifu Grand Hotel.

These *tokkuri-yashi* (*Mascarena lagenicaulis*), which look like bottles, are in Nagasakibana, southern Kyushu. Such plants draw much attention.

Haniwa Garden in Miyazaki is modeled after ancient burial mounds, and on display are replicas of *haniwa,* clay figures excavated from the mounds.

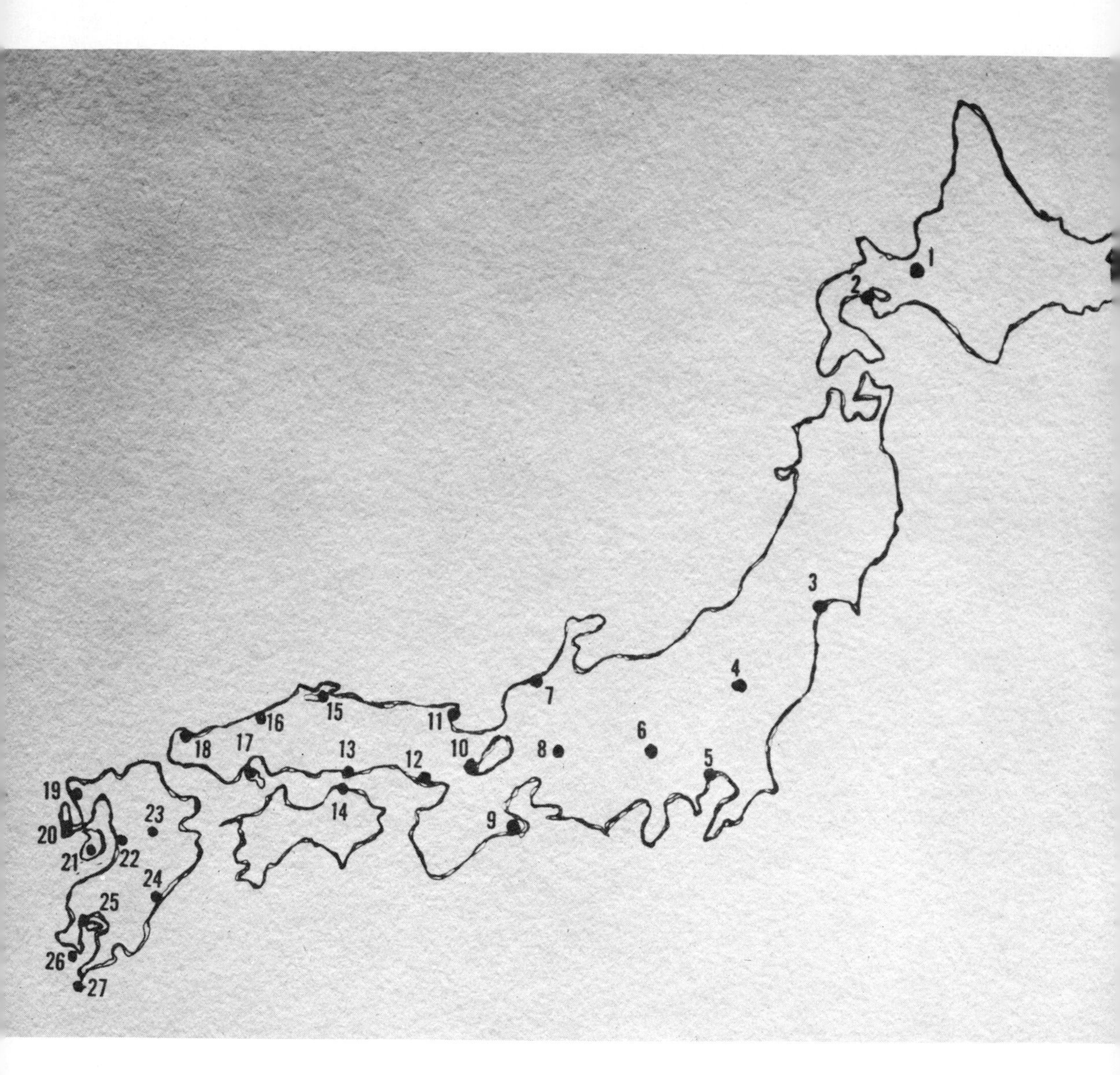
1
2
3
4
5
6
7
8
9
10
11
12
13
14
15
16
17
18
19
20
21
22
23
24
25
26
27

GLOSSARY OF PLACE NAMES

The map shows the location of places that are discussed in the text. The island at upper right is Hokkaido; the main island is Honshu; Kyushu lies southernmost; and the island between Honshu and Kyushu is Shikoku.

Amanohashidate 11
Aso Valley 23
Cape Sata 27
Chorakuen Hotel, Tamatsukuri near Matsue 15
Fujisan, or Mount Fuji, near Hakone 6
Fujiya Hotel, Hakone 6
Gifu Grand Hotel, Gifu 8
Ginza-Tokyu Hotel, Tokyo 5
Hakone 6
Heirinji, near Tokyo 5
Hotel Manseikaku, Lake Toya 2
Iko-zenji, Masuda 16
Iso Garden, Kagoshima 25
Izumo Plain, Matsue 15
Kagoshima 25
Kagoshima Bay 25
Kanazawa 7
Kashikojima 9
Kawatana 18
Kinashi-machi, Takamatsu 14
Kujukushima, near Sasebo 19
Kumamoto 22
Kyoto 10
Lake Toya 2
Masuda 16
Matsushima 3
Miyajima 17
Miyako Hotel, Kyoto 10
Miyanoshita, Hakone 6
Miyazaki 24
Mount Yotei, Lake Toya 2
Nagasaki 20
Nagasakibana 26
Nakajima Park, Sapporo 1
Nakanoshima, Lake Toya 2
Nikko 4
Okayama 13
Osaka 12
Sakurajima, Kagoshima 25
Sapporo 1
Sapporo Park Hotel, Sapporo 1
Sasebo 19
Shima Peninsula, Kashikojima 9
Shimabara, near Unzen 21
Takamatsu 14
Tamatsukuri, near Matsue 15
Tokyo 5
Toyako Spa, Lake Toya 2
Ujiyamada, Kashikojima 9
Unzen 21

Glossary

Here are brief explanations of the Japanese words used in this book. Many have no one-word English translation. They are quite easy to learn, and using them will bring you closer to understanding Japanese life.

aoki—*Aucuba japonica,* aucuba

chozubachi—a tall water basin, usually placed near an engawa

engawa—a narrow wooden platform at the wall line; it is a veranda, a porch, a stoop, an open corridor, or a balcony. The engawa can be any or all of these

fusuma—sliding interior wall panels

futon—Japanese bedding

genkan—entry vestibule

haniwa—cylindrical figures and tools excavated from ancient burial mounds

haran—*Aspidistra elatior,* "cast-iron plant"

hinoki—*Chamaecyparis obtusa,* Japanese cypress

hishaku—ladle

ibuki—*Juniperus chinesis,* Chinese juniper

ike—pond

kakehi—bamboo water pipe or flume

kame—tortoise

karesansui—dry landscape

kasuga-doro—kasuga type stone lantern, a tall hexagonal stone lantern

kaya—*Torreya nucifera*

kimono—article of Japanese apparel

kingyo—goldfish

koi—carp

kooen—parks

kotoji-toro—bridge-type stone lantern tern

kutsunugi-ishi—taking-off-shoes stone

machiai—waiting booth or chamber

maeishi—front stone

maki—*Podocarpus macrophyllus,* yew pine

masu—trout

matsu—pine

mokkoku—*Ternstroemia japonica*

nishiki-matsu—Japanese black pine with extraordinarily developed cork tissue around its trunk

nobedan—short paved walk

nokisudare—bamboo blind

nure-en—wet veranda, small veranda attached to an engawa

onko—(a kind of) *ichii, Taxus cuspidata,* Japanese yew

onsen—hot-spring spas

otera, tera—temples

ryokan—Japanese inns

ryoriya—Japanese restaurants

samurai—privileged military retainers

shoji—paper-covered sliding wall panels

sodegaki—a screen fence or sleeve fence

sozu—the "bam-boom"; a rocking bamboo pipe

sugi—Japanese cedar, or *Cryptomeria*

tanzaku—Japanese poem cards that are narrow and long

tanzaku-ishi—two stones cut in proportions similar to tanzakus, and laid in offset fashion to form a walk in a Japanese garden

tatami—straw mats, usually 3 by 6 feet, and about 2 inches thick, used to cover floors in Japanese houses

teshokuishi—a stone placed on the left of a water basin as a pedestal for a hand lantern

tokkuri-yashi—*Mascarena lagenicaulis*

tokonoma—an alcove where art treasures, objects, and/or flower arrangements are displayed

tsukubai—low water basin usually placed in a tea garden

tsuru—crane

tsuru-kame—a crane-tortoise combination

usu-ishi—millstone

yatsude—*Fatsia japonica; Aralia*

yukimi-doro—a low type of stone lantern with a large octagonal or round cap and light chamber; it stands on three or four legs

yutoseki—stone placed on the right of a water basin as a stand for a water container

zabuton—cushions laid directly on tatami

zashiki—the principal room in a Japanese house, a sort of all-purpose room

On special occasions Japanese ladies wear kimonos. Here, in Kanazawa, they are waiting for their turns to participate in the tea ceremony.

The Japanese people

The Japanese people today are much influenced by Western ideas. In most large cities the people wear Western clothes, enjoy Western cuisine, sleep in Western beds, and some have Western-style bathtubs. Most houses are equipped with modern conveniences. But nothing has become entirely Western, for Japan is a place where West meets East, and Western ideas are adapted to, and assimilated in harmony with, the traditional manner of living of the Japanese people.

That Japan is changing may seem obvious to a traveler. But most of the people still value highly their traditional way of life at work, in social gatherings, and at home. They bow graciously when they meet; they wear the *kimono* (especially on important occasions) and take their shoes off in the *genkan* (entry vestibule). At home they sit on *zabuton* (cushions) around a low table, sleep in *futon* laid directly on *tatami* mats, eat rice with chopsticks, and soak in a deep, hot Japanese tub.

The Japanese people like to travel. You can see families on tour and schoolchildren on field trips all over Japan. Newlyweds take honeymoon trips. Almost all carry cameras, and when they return they bring home souvenirs. Many people visit the large cities, where they find much to interest them. Other preferred places are *onsen* (hot-spring spas) where one may soak in hot springs, relax, and forget the mundane world.

In Kyushu and along the coast bordering the Sea of Japan, we found little of the Western influence. People there still live in the traditional Japanese way.

The Japanese house

One characteristic of the Japanese house is that the floor is considerably above ground level. When we enter a typical Japanese house, we find a genkan, or entry vestibule, where we are welcomed and where we take off our shoes or footwear. Then we step upon a platform that is the floor of the house itself. Rooms have tatami mat floors and *fusuma* (sliding interior panels) that partition off the rooms. (For more about Japanese interiors, see our earlier book *The Japanese House . . . Its Interior and Exterior.*) Most *zashiki* (the principal rooms in Japanese houses) face the garden; some have an *engawa* (a narrow platform or veranda) outside; some do not; but on one side of the zashiki there is always the *tokonoma* (alcove). Usually there are no chairs, except that in recent years chairs may be placed on the engawa. A large low table is usually placed in the room for dining and various diversions. A Japanese room is a versatile affair that is used for different daily activities. It may serve as a living room, drawing room, dining room, or bedroom. *Futon* (Japanese bedding) is brought out of a closet at night and put back in the morning.

Although there are some fixed partitions, Japanese interiors are generally separated by fusuma; when you want to look out, or when more light is needed, there are *shoji,* or sliding translucent panels. Living space is flexible. By removing or adding partitions, and by closing or opening shoji or fusuma, rooms can be made larger and smaller.

On the outside, wooden panels, insect screens, glass doors, and often a combination of glass and shoji all slide on tracks and serve various purposes. Shoji can be

A view from the garden, looking at the zashiki, or principal room. A little bamboo engawa, or platform, and the bottom of the sliding shoji show the floor line of the house. The halves of two shoji in the center are lifted for a view of the garden. The house is in Kyoto.

pushed back partially or completely or can be closed for privacy and diffused light. Glass doors provide a view of gardens and keep out the wind. The exterior sliding wooden panels are drawn and locked at night, in rainy or stormy weather, or for protection during absence from the home.

With few exceptions, the Japanese house has a garden wall, fence, or hedge on the property line to enclose the lot, and a gate or gates provide entry. The building may stand at one corner or in the center of the lot. The gate will open upon a path that leads to the main entry. This area is generally separate from the main garden, which can be best viewed from the zashiki. Generally, the interior of the property is so arranged that it cannot be seen from the other houses or from the street. The Japanese house and garden are fenced in to exclude the busy outside world and to ensure a maximum of privacy.

Traditional Japanese gardens

You may find traditional Japanese gardens at private residences, at *ryokan* (inns), *ryoriya* (restaurants), and villas; at historic mansions, palaces, and castles; at *otera* (temples) and shrines; in *kooen* (parks); and at former residences of *samurai* (privileged military retainers).

Gardens in good residential areas are secluded by high fences, tall gates, and dense plantings, which make them impossible to be seen from the street. The residences or villas of prominent families invariably have good gardens. In fact, such houses may have several gardens: an entrance garden, inner garden, main garden, and tea garden.

Space is at a premium in Japan, but private residences of wealthy families can provide such space; and to use it wisely and artfully, professionals are often consulted concerning design and maintenance. Old family gardens that have received exceptionally good care over the years are elaborately maintained.

Also, as masters of the art of flower arrangement, the tea ceremony, and other traditional aspects of their culture, the Japanese tend to have good gardens for their professional use and personal enjoyment. Tea gardens are inseparable from the tea houses or the tea ceremony.

Ryokan, or Japanese inns, and some Western hotels maintain traditional gardens that enable one to live closely with natural beauty. Such gardens are an integral part of the buildings, and are designed as harmonious complements.

Ryoriya are traditional Japanese restaurants for dining and entertainment; usually it is necessary to make a reservation, for dining and entertainment may take an entire night. The sizes of their gardens vary, but generally they are elaborately designed.

An otera is a Buddist temple where people go to worship. A temple may be a large building or it may be quite humble in size. The priests' quarters are usually adjacent to the main temple building, and may also have traditional gardens.

Gardens at historic sites represent the best of earlier periods, and are compositions by famous garden designers.

Though samurai were warriors, they also pursued cultural and intellectual interests in ancient times, and created original gardens. Today, though the samurai are long gone, their descendants have kept their spirit alive in their gardens.

Kooen, or parks, may be found in any city or town. Some are famous historic sites, and are usually gardens through which one may stroll.

Traditional gardens may be found wherever you go in Japan. But just because you know where they are does not necessarily mean that you may visit them at any time. To enter some private residences, ryoriya (unless you dine), and historic places it is necessary to have permission or an introduction by an acquaintance. You may visit otera, shrines, parks, and other public places during certain hours. There are few samurai houses in existence, but you may occasionally come across one unexpectedly. We saw only two on our trip, one in Nikko and the other in Kanazawa.

The Japanese house and garden are designed together

Japanese gardens and Japanese houses are designed together. Because the zashiki is the most important room in the house, the garden is designed to be viewed and admired from this room. Most owners design their properties with trees, shrubs, rocks, and ornaments artfully planted with a care for perspective, to give a feeling of distance, and perhaps with a waterfall or a pond to lend an air of spaciousness and to create greater interest.

The design of the garden usually indicates why plants and ornamental objects are placed at particular sites. There may be *kutsunugi-ishi* (taking-off-shoes stone) outside the zashiki, and steppingstones or a path that leads from one point of interest to another. Lantern, rocks, and special plantings are generally included.

Sometimes there is a *sodegaki* (screen fence) outside the zashiki. When you look from the room, you see only the lovely vista of the garden, with any uninteresting sight screened by the sodegaki, which is usually accented by means of plants, rocks, and/or ornaments.

From outside the zashiki, a path may lead to the garden area, the side, or back of the house, to another garden or to the entrance area to the main house. Here there is usually a gate or something that suggests a gate. Usually the traditional detached Japanese house has a wall, fence, or hedge on the property line together with a gate. The gate opens upon a garden pathway that leads to the entry. From the gate to the entry is a separate garden area that usually is simple in design. The main entrance gate or gates are usually sturdily built, and may be elaborate, but the plants, rocks, and other ornamental objects in this area are usually quite modest in plan and execution.

For a detailed look at the various parts that are brought together to create the Japanese garden, you may want to consult our earlier book *The Art of the Japanese Garden.*

A traditional Japanese house with thatched roof, in Kumamoto. The hedge fences in the property. Underneath the shaped trees lies the garden.

Garden design: the short view and the long

Nature has always been the predominant influence in the design of Japanese houses and gardens. In traditional garden designs two factors are basic: first, the use of the best natural features and topographical variations of the lot, and, second, the most effective utilization of distant scenery, if any, so that it may be successfully incorporated in the background of the total design—as "borrowed scenery," so to speak.

Nature as seen in a Japanese garden can be a replica of countryside, coast, or forest. The design usually calls for a flat area close to the house, with an artificial hill in the background that is used for a planting area. A waterfall, waterway, pond, lanterns, or water basin may be placed to add interest. A fence and gate separate the garden areas.

Sometimes you may find a flat garden simply composed of just a few rocks or rocks used together with plants and sand. Rocks or rock arrangements may represent a complex idea, but more commonly they symbolize an island or islands in the ocean, a sea of white sand, or mountains and water. They are very neat in appearance, and have their own special beauty and atmosphere.

In many dry gardens, rocks symbolize mountains, and courses of stones are used to depict waterfalls and flowing streams. However, some dry gardens are completely abstract in design, and create a contemplative mood.

The tearoom and garden may be attached to the main house or, in rustic surroundings, may be altogether detached. The planning of the tea garden usually follows formal rules.

Japanese parks and public places are usually of large dimensions. Naturally, the designs are not quite like those of a home or ryokan, but provide extensive vistas and areas in which to walk.

Although traditional Japanese gardens usually can be said to represent a certain style, they are also naturally composed to some degree, and therefore have a basic similarity. Yet no two gardens are ever the same, for each has characteristics that reveal the taste of the owner and the designer.

Water in the garden

Water, plants, and rock or stones are the three basic elements in a Japanese garden. In design, the appearance of artificiality is avoided, while natural forms and elements are used so artfully that the planned garden will look unplanned. The presence of water is all-important, and is emphasized as much as possible in all landscaped Japanese gardens. It may be in the form of actual water or simulated by arrangements of sand, pebbles, or stones in dry watercourses.

The *ike* (pond) may represent the sea, a lake, a pond, or a river in nature. The shape is usually irregular, and from any viewpoint all its curves and borders are never completely revealed. A stream flowing into a pond is usually bordered with natural stones, wood, and various plants.

In *karesansui* (dry landscape), a waterfall may be suggested by a tall stone, while sand, gravel, or pebbles, positioned with infinite care, may symbolize a stream.

This is a natural stream, both sides of which are bordered with rocks of varying sizes.

This is a man-made stream that, even though it is an artificial creation, has a strong natural effect. Note the similarities between the two photographs.

Green in the garden

Because of Japan's mild climate, foliage is luxuriant and the choice of plant materials seems almost limitless. Though regional species are seen, the principal trees used in Japanese gardens are evergreens, primarily conifers. *Matsu* (pine), *sugi* (Japanese cedar, or *Cryptomeria*), *ibuki* (Chinese juniper), *hinoki* (*Chamaecyparis obtusa*), *maki* (yew pine, or *Podocarpus macrophyllus*), *kaya* (*Torreya nucifera*), holly, varieties of broadleaf evergreens, bamboo, maple, cherry, plum, camellia, magnolia, azalea, fern, *haran* ("cast-iron plant," *Aspidistra elatior*), *yatsude* (*Fatsia japonica, Aralia*), mondo grass, and moss are most often seen. Most of them are available in the United States. Where they are not, you can usually make substitutions to achieve similar effects.

Using the shades and the nuances of the evergreens, a mixture of greens is preferred in the Japanese garden. A profusion of bright color and flowers is not the idea; only a dash of seasonal color is preferred. One proportion is 7 to 3; that is, 7 evergreens for 3 deciduous trees. But in many gardens the percentage of evergreens is much higher.

When a new garden is landscaped, almost all the plants are brought in from nurseries, even large trees. Therefore poles are used to brace the trees until the roots of the large ones take firm hold. The poles also help to maintain the desired shapes.

The Japanese take good care of the plants in their gardens. They shape the trees according to their liking, and control the shape and size of the plants so that they remain healthy and appear to the best advantage in their setting. A pine, for instance, receives attention twice a year. In the spring, the new shoots are pinched; and later, in the autumn or winter, old needles are removed.

To make compact, ground-hugging azaleas, shaping should begin when they are young, and should be maintained each season. Trim the contour of the azaleas gradually, into the desired low shape. Once the shape has been established, trim the plant just after blooming is finished or even when it is flowering; it will bear even more flowers in the next season.

A Japanese gardener trims and shapes most plants at any time of the year. Flowering plants are trimmed or pruned before they bear buds so that they will produce flowers in the coming season. Japanese gardeners use hedge shears to trim most small-leaf plants, and pruning shears for large-leaf plants. If hedge shears are used on the latter, the half-cut leaves will remain on the tree, and the effect is not pleasing to the eye.

In Japan we saw many beautifully shaped maki (yew pine). At home, in San Francisco, we rarely see them.

In Kyoto and other places, we saw sugi (Japanese cedar) in a pompon shape, as well as some bamboos cut similarly. The shaped sugi and the bamboo must be trimmed to maintain their forms. Bamboos are used in different areas of the gardens both naturally and trimmed. When new shoots come out, unwanted ones should be removed.

We saw rather dark juniper in odd forms in Kyushu. They were shaped in large pompons, and many were used as hedges because of their exotic natural shapes and beautiful deep-green color.

In Japan, when you see well-shaped trees from the street, you can almost always be sure that the house has a well-cared-for garden.

A path beside the house, with trees and shrubs on both sides, bare rock, smooth steppingstones, and a sweep of gravel surface, all give an air of peace and quiet to this dwelling.

Stone is all-important

Stones, rocks, and their arrangements are most important in all Japanese gardens. They are liberally used either realistically or symbolically. As symbols they may represent mountains, waterfalls, streams, a crane or tortoise, or even boats and islands in the sea. Rocks and stones in groups or in a mass are used in garden construction to hold soil, for architectural foundations, as stairs, and for paths.

Stones and rocks are the framework of the garden, and the interest of the design depends on their use and decorativeness. Sometimes a single stone or rock is a pure accent; but for the most part, carefully selected and placed stones and rocks serve two purposes in Japanese gardens—practicality and ornamentation.

You will see stone in Japanese gardens in many sizes, shapes, colors, and textures. It may be used in its natural forms, or as cut or crushed stone. The designer selects stones of a size, shape, color, and texture to harmonize with other elements of the garden. He uses sand, gravel, pebbles, crushed and small stones for ground covers, for paths, and in or near watercourses or water areas.

Large stones are used to hold soil—in a retaining wall, along the banks of a stream or pond, by the sides of a path. They are also placed as to complement trees, plants, or other ornamental objects.

Flat stones or slabs are used for steppingstones and across narrow streams. You will also see carved and hewn stone, stone cut as lanterns, water basins, and used for pagodas and bridges.

A typical kasuga-doro, or tall stone lantern, at the side of a path, with a few steppingstones leading up to it.

The role of ornaments

Japanese gardens usually contain ornamental objects: lanterns, water basins, bridges, natural rocks, pagodas, figures—all of which serve as accents or points of especial interest.

Stone lanterns

A stone lantern is made of carved stone parts that are put together to look like a lantern. If you saw the disassembled pieces, you might not recognize them for what they are. It is said that the first use of lanterns in gardens was by tea masters

The yukimi-doro, or low stone lantern, which is usually, but not always, placed near water on a rock.

who borrowed dedication lanterns from old temples and shrines to ornament their tea gardens. They were originally used to provide light, but today they have no practical use at all, and are simply decoration.

In general they are of two styles: one, slim and tall in appearance; the other, low and somewhat broad. The typical tall lantern is called *kasuga doro,* and it may be placed at the side of a path, in an entry area, near a water basin, or on a hill. It is usually set in shadowy or off-the-way sites, rather than full view, with a tree for background or beneath a drooping branch. The low, flat lantern is called *yukimi-doro* (snow-viewing lantern), and is generally placed near water or on the shoreline of a pond or stream. There are many other types of lantern, as well as derivations of these two styles.

Iron lanterns, which are ornamental and charming, are used on top of a low stone in smaller landscapes, such as in the entry garden or beside a path, and are also hung from the eave at the corner of a building.

Wooden lanterns are made mostly (but not always) of bamboo, and are often seen at the side of a path. They can also be placed near a pond.

You may place lanterns anywhere you wish, as there is no set rule governing them except that of aesthetics and use.

This is a tsukubai (water basin).

Water basins

Water basins are chiefly of stone, natural, hewn, or cut to shape; rarely of ceramic, pottery, or metal.

Stone water basins come in two types. The tall kind, called *chozubachi,* is placed near the engawa of a building. Often, sodegaki is used as its background. The other is *tsukubai.* Tsukubai is a low-silhouette water basin placed at stooping height, and is almost always accompanied by a *kakehi* (bamboo pipe or flume) that carries water to the basin. It is usually seen in tea gardens.

The shape and size of the water basin reflect one's personal fancy. There are traditional ways of placing the basin and its accompanying group of stones, as well as the steppingstones that lead up to it. A stone lantern usually stands nearby for illumination. The basin has a concave area in the center to hold water for rinsing the mouth and hands. On top of the water basin is usually placed a *hishaku,* (ladle) for scooping up the water.

One of the most interesting aspects of the water basin is its use in the formal tea ceremony. Usually the area is laid out in a traditional pattern, though no two such places are exactly the same. The water basin is set in a hollow spot surrounded by a group of irregular stones. In the center of the hollow, which is of clay or concrete, is a hole for drainage, and over the hole pebbles arc piled. The hollow area is sometimes covered entirely by pebbles. In front of the water basin is a large flat stone, called a *maeishi,* up to which steppingstones lead. At the left is a stone (*teshokuishi*) that once served to hold a lantern. The right-hand stone (*yutoseki*) is for the water container. The stone lantern serves to light the scene.

This is a chozubachi (water basin).

This is a tsukubai at the foot of a rock wall. Notice how simple the materials are and how casual the placement is.

This is a typical bamboo inner gate and fence dividing garden areas. They are usually constructed of very light materials. This garden is underneath the shaped trees seen on page 23.

Next to the shoji, or white sliding door, is a wooden sodegaki, or screen fence. Note the height of the house floor above ground level. The large stone is a kutsunugi-ishi, or taking-off-shoes stone.

Gates and fences

For their living quarters, the Japanese insist on privacy. Therefore gates and fences play important roles in garden design, and they are constructed with great imagination. At most homes a gate and fence enclose the property. Inside, quite often an inner gate or fence divides areas such as the entrance area from the main garden.

The sleeve fence

A sodegaki is a short screenlike fence. It is literally called a "sleeve fence" because of its resemblance to the sleeve of a kimono. It is a useful partition that begins directly at the house wall, organizes space, and creates different views from the interior rooms. It can be made of dry bamboo or of a combination of two or three different wooden materials. It may also be composed of plants that are grown to serve the function of a screening wall or partition. When you sit indoors and look out, the sodegaki is artfully placed to give you a beautiful view of a carefully chosen segment of the garden.

Many-storied pagodas

A stone pagoda has more religious significance than a mere charming piece of garden ornament, for in the Orient pagodas are the temples of divinities. The highest pagoda is thirteen stories. They come in variations of three, five, seven, nine, and thirteen stories. A pagoda is usually placed on higher ground or on a hillside toward the rear of the garden, visible from any position.

Visiting some Japanese gardens

The jumbled rocks and stones of any river bottom or mountain have little meaning or value until they are brought into a garden and carefully assembled there, where they acquire new meaning and value as they express the thought of the designer of the garden. The pictures in this book were chosen to reveal, both in details and in overall settings, the ways in which many different Japanese gardeners have applied their ideas to various materials to create superb gardens.

This creek is the continuation of the stream seen in the right-hand picture. The gravel-covered path leads to the steppingstone, to the stone in the stream, to another steppingstone on the opposite bank, and continues on.

A waterfall starts from the top of a tall boulder. Between the low rock in the middle ground and the rock on the center left runs a stream. The gravel area in the foreground is the path, and to the left is the scene in the left-hand picture.

Alongside the irises and massive rock runs the stream, curving gently along the edge of the rock. At the start of the stream, on higher ground, the water flows faster, as may be seen in the center of this photograph.

The large stone on the bank of the stream is surrounded by ferns, azaleas, and pine to suggest a natural feeling. On the hill are shaped azaleas. Directly above the yatsude (*Fatsia japonica*) is the waterfall area (the upper-right picture on the opposite page).

The large garden of a ryoriya

One of the most popular garden styles is that which simulates nature—a combination of an artificial mountain bordered by a stream-fed pond, a flat area, a mounded rise, which is often a planting area, together with a waterfall, stream, pond, and ornamental objects. Such a garden provides a splendid view from any angle, and expresses the originality of the designer. Characteristically, such gardens are fenced in. Thick stands of trees and a fence or wall exclude the outside world.

This is the garden of a ryoriya (Japanese restaurant). The natural scenic features are beautifully arranged, without the clutter of ornament one sometimes sees in a restaurant or hotel garden. On the next ten pages you will see steppingstones in the stream, a bridge, a sodegaki, a gate, and trimmed bamboos.

View of the main garden

The size of the garden on these two pages is about 35 feet in width and 40 feet in depth. The entire property extends about 15 feet to each side of this view. From the left a little creek runs down to the front of the yukimi-doro (snow-viewing stone lantern) area, where a pond is located. The rear is a planting area. The cir-

The right-side view of the garden on page 35. Compare the low pine leaning over the stream with the photograph on page 35.

cular planting space in front of the yukimi-doro, which is across the stream, is about 10 feet in diameter. (See next page.) In back of the yukimi-doro and the trees is a house with a tile roof. You may see these on page 44. The stream runs beside the small house on the right, and there are steppingstones on which to cross the stream. Close-ups of this section are on pages 40-41.

1. In front of the clump of iris is a little watercourse that separates the flower bed from the lawn. The trimmed azaleas on the left are part of the mounded planting area.

Stone bridge and steppingstones along a stream

2. Here, well-placed steppingstones, avoiding a straight line, lead to a slightly curved stone bridge.

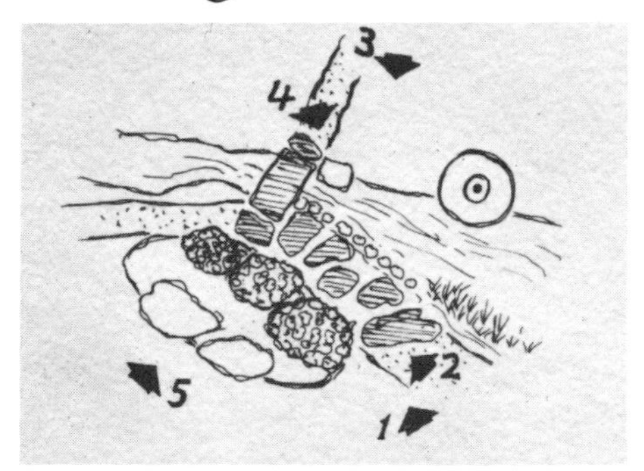

Numbers show the places from which the photographs were taken. No. 5 shows the direction whence the picture on the previous page was taken.

3. This view is from the garden side, looking at the lawn and the main building. To the center right, above the steppingstones, is the round planting area occupied by groupings of azaleas and stones. In back of the lantern are a pond and irises.

4. A close-up of the bridge and steppingstones, shown in Picture 2, but from the other side. Here you can see how steppingstones are placed in a flowing stream, while irregularly placed stones border the pond, which contains some friendly *koi* (carp).

This view is from the lawn side, looking toward the garden and cottage. This part is on the right side of the house on page 37. Here a path leads both to the left and to the right, and crosses the stream by means of steppingstones.

Steppingstones in a stream

Running water can be the chief element of interest in a garden if you make it the way Nature herself might have created it. These two pages show the same area from different angles. This little creek originates in the pond on page 39.

This is a close-up of the center area in the upper picture. The gravel path leads to the creek, where the stone on the right is the first of the steppingstones. Two stones stand in flowing water, while the other two are placed partially in the water and partially on the ground, thus bridging the two sides.

Japanese gardens always have focal points of interest. In this area it is the steppingstones crossing the stream. Here a large, protruding stone cuts the even flow and width of the creek, not quite zigzag, but making the stream bed narrow and wide, and the water shallow and deep. Two steppingstones in the water divide the tiny ravine into three parts. The materials used are stones of different sizes and various kinds of plants, but the steppingstones unite the whole tiny land- and water-scape.

This is a view opposite that of the picture on the previous page. Here the water runs from lower right to upper left. Because the large steppingstone is partially embedded in the ground, the watercourse narrows around the outer point of the stone.

Inner gate, fence, and sodegaki

Left: The large stone on left front is called the kutsunugi-ishi (taking-off-shoes stone). It leads down to the stepping-stones set in moss, and on to the simple bamboo gate. The white panel at the extreme left of the picture is a shoji. The dark block between the shoji and the tall bamboo sodegaki is the door box for sliding wooden exterior panels that are closed at night. The dark pebbles under the eaves are practical as well as decorative because they keep that area and house wall free of rain and dirt. The sodegaki, gate, and fence are made of bamboo and sugi poles.

A sodegaki always starts from a building. This elaborate one is quite long in order to screen the rooms on the opposite side. On this side of the sodegaki, azaleas, maple, stone, pine, and nandina also add to the screening effect.

Three short granite columns, two on the left and one on the right, together with large low natural stone and plants, make a gate for this path, and also serve a decorative purpose.

On each side of a gravel path stand bamboos with their branches pruned short. Here smaller granite columns are repeated as fencing. The path leads around the sugi bark fence to the scene in the upper picture.

A cedar pole, magnolia, and two granite columns suggest a sodegaki. The pole (dark) upholds trellises of wisteria. These stone columns are similar to those on the previous page.

Sodegaki with an open feeling

This open, airy type of sodegaki is used so that, when the glass doors are open, guests can view the garden, and the presence of the sodegaki is unobtrusive.

Japanese rooms are measured according to the number of tatami mats that fit into them. The size of a mat is usually 3 by 6 feet, and rooms are 3, 4½, 6, 8, 10, 12 or more mats in size. By removing the *fusuma* (sliding interior wall panels) that separate most Japanese rooms, an 8-mat room can be incorporated with an adjoining 12-mat room in order to accommodate a large group. When the fusuma are removed, you can see the garden from inside without obstruction because the sodegaki is airy, and a part of the garden. When rooms are separated by fusuma, such an airy sodegaki serves to create two vistas, as well as a feeling of privacy.

On the right, where the drapery meets a beam, are the fusuma that close off the adjoining room.

Garden interests—haran

A close-up of steppingstones, one natural squarish stone and two long cut stones called *tanzaku-ishi* (poem-card stones), in reference to the writing of poems on similarly proportioned paper called *tanzaku*. They are laid in the overlapping position that is traditional in Japan. In the rear of the stones, actually the side of the garden, haran (aspidistra), holly, gold-leaf plant, and nandina are planted for decoration and to hide the bottom of the fence.

This is the left-side view of the garden on page 34. At this corner of the house, a gravel path leads to another part of the garden and around the house. Haran are planted at the corner of house for two reasons: to decorate and to designate a corner.

Garden of otera, Iko-zenji, Masuda

Masuda is a small city on the coast of the Sea of Japan. We made a special trip to visit this outstanding garden. (See map, page 14.)

Sesshu (1420–1506), the greatest artist of his period, a priest as well as an artist and garden designer, became the fifth resident priest of this little otera (temple) on the coast in the fifteenth century. During his residence, five centuries ago, he designed this garden.

The garden is backed by a natural hill. On the slope and at the foot of the hill are various trimmed shrubs. This garden is called the Garden of Tsuru-kame (crane-tortoise) because it contains a stone arrangement indicating a *tsuru* (crane) and a stone island representing

The garden pictured on these last pages is designed to be viewed from various points of vantage, while sitting in a room or strolling along the paths; even small areas and corners have their special pictorial qualities.

Above: This view is from a zashiki, looking out upon the garden of tsuru-kame. "Sit here and enjoy this garden," the attendant told us. One shoji is drawn open.

Right: In this view you see the kutsunugi-ishi and engawa; the shoji is closed. The second panel from the far end was opened for the picture above.

Three shoji have been drawn back. This view is seen from the same position as in the top photograph on the opposite page.

a *kame* (tortoise). Furthermore, when viewed from the main hall, the pond has the shape of a flying crane. As both tsuru and kame are symbols of longevity, this has indeed been a celebrated garden for more than 450 years.

Notice that all the stones have strong outlines and that there is an absence of smooth edges. Sesshu's paintings are recognized by their strong lines and virility. The same characteristics are reflected in this garden, which includes a waterfall, pond, hill, island, and flat area. The garden may be viewed from any part of the engawa.

The area is fenced in by trees, mountainside, and buildings, and can be seen only from the rooms. The idea of secluding a garden by means of fencing is common in most traditional Japanese homes, although the arrangement of house, garden space, and environment may make the effect different in each one, lending it individuality.

The garden materials used here are simply stones and plants; there are no ornaments. The shapes of the plants and shrubs are said to be very much the same as they were five centuries ago.

From the zashiki. The space between the shoji and the sliding glass doors is the engawa. You can see part of the steppingstones, a large, smooth stone, trimmed plants, a fence, and a neighbor's plants in back of the fence.

A traditional Japanese family garden

The above picture shows how zashiki and garden relate to each other. As you see, the garden is really an extension of the room. If the glass doors were closed you would not see the steppingstones, but your eyes would be drawn upward, and you could still see the garden. In this picture you cannot see the sodegaki placed to the left of the glass door. This is not a large or decorative garden, but a quiet, intimate family area containing traditional garden ideas.

On the engawa, a rug or tatami mat covering (as you see here) may be spread to give a warm feeling; there may also be a table and chairs for convenience. The

This view is of the left side of the photograph on the previous page. Notice the light framework sodegaki. Stones, plants, and silky maple form an additional natural sodegaki, making this area more interesting. Steppingstones lead around the house.

This is to the right of the photograph on the previous page. Shrubs against the wall suggest a sodegaki, while steppingstones lead to the kutsu-nugi-ishi, which in turn leads to another room. The stones also continue on beyond, to the tall water basin.

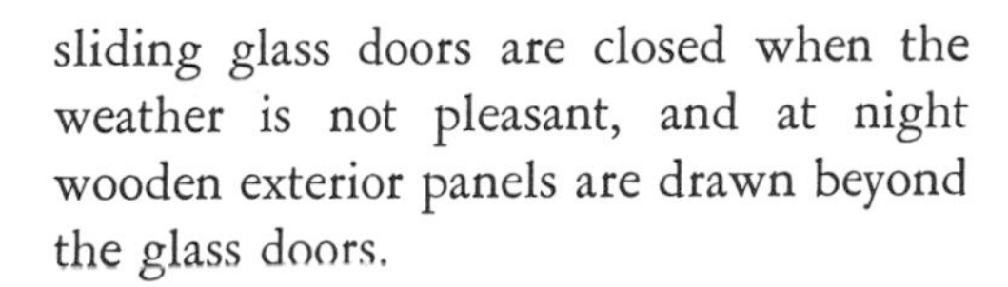

sliding glass doors are closed when the weather is not pleasant, and at night wooden exterior panels are drawn beyond the glass doors.

This garden belongs to our longtime friend Mr. Shuho Sato, who gives it the best of care. Every morning he himself waters it, and prunes the trees whenever necessary. The soil is natural, and there is not a single weed.

The steppingstones viewed from above the zashiki. Notice how the shrubs soften the corner, and the interesting layout of the stones. The soil creates the illusion of water.

Garden path beside a house

In this long, narrow passage area, the steppingstones and nobedan (short paved walk) are laid out artistically to provide an interesting approach to the building. At the center left, a camellia and rock suggest a sodegaki. To the right of the mondo grass in the center is a water basin, a close-up of which is on the next page. To the right is the planting area; the rest of the surface is covered by gravel, a type of ground covering that has a crisp feeling, and keeps both the inside and outside of the house clean.

The rock at the foot of the camellia on the preceding page shows its rough surface to the right of the paved walk, where haran are planted at the side for a feeling of greater naturalness.

In placing a rock, the Japanese designer will bury a good part of it—not only to make it secure but also to make it seem as if the rock had been there for many years. An appearance of instability is regarded as a weakness, and is altogether avoided in garden construction.

The water-basin area as seen from the zashiki.

The Japanese call this short paved walk a nobedan. This one is divided into seven angular parts by rows of inset pebbles. The dark stones, of course, add decoration. To make a path different, a combination of nobedan, of various designs, with steppingstones is often used.

This is the left side of the main entry. The shoji door is another entrance to the house. Between the two entries is a moss-covered circular planting area in which grow a maple and short bamboos. The steppingstones provide an approach to the second entrance.

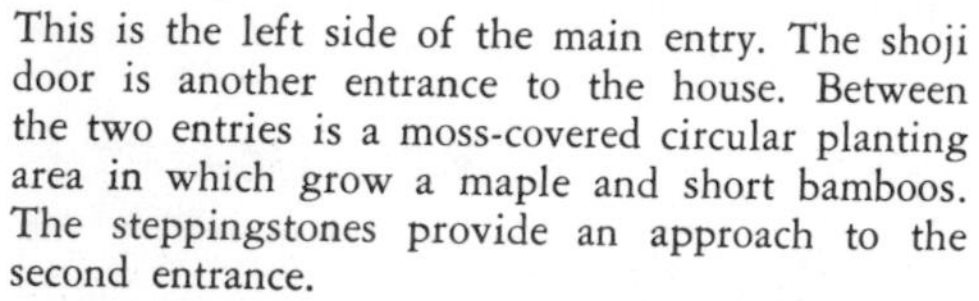

White gravel is spread to both sides of the path. The curved planting area is mounded slightly higher than the gravel surface. Sugi and maples back the stone lantern at the edge of the gravel. Note how the maple leans toward the lantern, shading it slightly from one's view.

From the street the paved pathway leads to the main entrance. A sodegaki and short bamboos lead you in. The other two pictures on this page are of the left side, and the two photographs on the opposite page are of the right side of this main path.

A sophisticated entrance garden

The entrance garden is an important complement to the house. Though small in area compared to the main garden, it is the first one seen, and should reflect the mood and spirit of the home.

This is the entrance garden of a ryoriya. Because many guests will enter and leave, the area is somewhat larger than that of an ordinary family house, and the paved walk is wider for the same reason. On each side of the pathway

Near the right of the entrance is a low stone lantern shadowed by short bamboos and *aoki* (aucuba).

This pleasant section is at the right side of the path, near the street. The dark area at the bottom is natural soil along the fence that borders the property. Here, pruned bamboos are grouped; unwanted growth will be removed to maintain the classic simplicity of the design.

leading to the main entry, plants and ornaments are arranged simply and neatly, yet in a very sophisticated manner. The area is completely enclosed, and nothing of the neighbor's property can be seen. Before guests arrive, the garden is lightly watered, giving it a fresh and welcoming scent.

Bamboo is one of the favorite materials used in Japanese gardens, and this one is no exception. There are many different kinds of bamboo: tall, medium, bushy, large, and narrow-leafed and black-stemmed. All require water, but it is easy to keep them healthy. The Japanese prune their bamboos to make pompons or to thin out the branches. When new shoots come up, all are studied, and both old and new ones are removed to keep the area simple and uncrowded. In this entrance area, you can see one way of trimming, thinning, and grouping bamboos.

An attractive entrance garden

Alongside a paved pathway a large natural stone embedded in the ground gives the impression of great age. Between the bamboo fence and the stone are carefully grouped short and tall plants that give depth to this tiny area.

Left: In this view, an artfully arranged pathway, which is more practical and convenient than steppingstones, is laid between the front gate and the main entry to the house. The parking area is outside the gate. Note the shaped, aged maki in front of the vertical grilled wall, and the stone, a close-up of which appears in the upper picture.

This view is from the entry area, looking outward on the paved path and on the circular planting where stones and well-trimmed shrubs are gathered harmoniously.

Here we look from the stone area in the upper photograph on the last page. The pathway from the front gate ends here, facing a small, well-planted section. To the left is the guest entry to the house. The pathway to the right is a separate entrance for daily use by family, servants, and tradesmen.

A path, bordered by a flowing brook, leads around the corner of the house. From a handsome wood arch an iron lantern is suspended over the path.

This lantern hanging at the corner of a house is actually lighted, creating a delicate mood.

The slant of the top of this lantern, and the slope of its sides, almost repeat the angle of the corner of the eaves from which it is suspended, and add an exquisite feeling to the area.

Japanese hanging lanterns

Most Japanese hanging lanterns are small, about 5 to 8 inches by 10 to 12 inches in size, and their shapes vary. Most are made of iron, bamboo, or wood. Some are ceramic, but these are usually not hung.

The hanging lanterns are both practical and decorative. They are often suspended from the eaves.

The handsome lanterns in these two pages serve to dress up the areas and create a mood.

Wooden lanterns in the garden

The Japanese use both hanging lanterns and pillarless lanterns as ornamental objects in their gardens. The styles are similar, consisting mainly of the cap and the light chamber. Most of these lanterns have no pillars. Originally they were used to illuminate the garden. Keeping that primary idea in mind, today they are placed where light may be needed, such as near the entrance or at the side of a path, on a wooden stand or on a rock, or hung or suspended.

Even when they are not lighted, they are still charming decorations.

On this page a wooden lantern sits on a wooden pillar beside a bridge, and another on a rock along a path.

Lanterns on rocks

Pillarless lanterns can be hung unless they are of great weight, and hanging lanterns can also be variously placed in gardens as pillarless lanterns. On this page are four different types of hanging or pillarless lanterns. Because they are rather small, they must be placed carefully so that they will be in scale with nearby plants, stones, and other garden materials.

One of the two most-used water basins is of low silhouette, set in a hollow area with a group of stones, as in the photograph. The hishaku (ladle) is placed over the basin; a bamboo pipe carries spring water; and a stone lantern illuminates the area. This is a typical tea-garden arrangement.

Another greatly used water basin, larger and taller, is usually placed near the engawa, on a rock. Here the vertical pipe and feed pipe are of the same size, and are close to the basin.

This water basin sits at the water's edge. The feed pipe begins behind the rock; the vertical pipe is hidden. A water basin can also be placed at the side of a path or near the entrance to a home.

Bamboo pipe for water basin

A water basin is almost always fed by a bamboo pipe. Although there are various ways to set it up and shape the end of it, the bamboo pipe, or kakehi, is simply a length of whole or split bamboo. The end of the feed pipe is about 4 to 10 inches above the waterline and the center of the basin. The water may be allowed to drip continuously through the pipe or it may be turned on and off. The length of the feed pipe is optional, but its length should be harmonious with its environment.

In the picture below, the bamboo pipe seems to come through the sodegaki. But the cluster of slender vertical bamboo branches, of the same material as the sodegaki in the background, is really the covering for a vertical water pipe. This water basin is set close to an engawa.

Bamboo feed pipe

The picture above shows a long bamboo feed pipe following the side of a stone lantern and supported by two small bamboo sticks. This is another typical tea-garden water basin and its surroundings.

The picture on the right shows a long bamboo standpipe tied with string, the T-joint of the pipe, and a long waterfall from the pipe to the basin. This arrangement was in an entry corner.

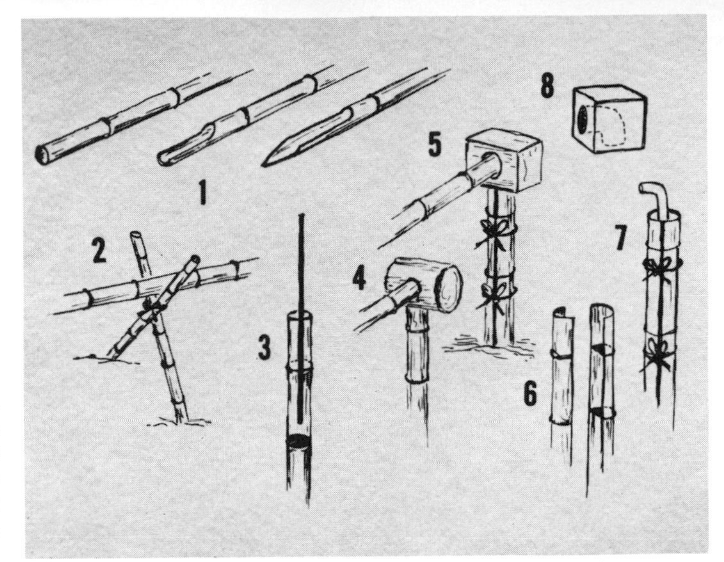

The bamboo water pipe, a garden accessory made of bamboo and wood, is a charming way to bring water into the basin. The principle of the bamboo water pipe is always the same, but it can be made in many different ways. The sketches show examples.

How to assemble a feed pipe

1. Different shapes for the end of the feed pipe. The size and length vary.
2. Support for the bamboo pipe. If the bamboo pipe is long, you can use two or more supports.
3. Metal rod to remove bamboo joints so the water will flow through.
4. The T-joint block can be one section of bamboo, a 4-by-4-inch block, or a piece of log.
5. Insert feed pipe and vertical pipe into T-joint block.
6. For the vertical pipe, split bamboo in half with a knife or hatchet, and take the inside joints out so that the bamboo walls can enclose the pipe (or hose).
7. Place the split bamboo halves around the metal pipe, and tie them with string. The hook-shaped pipe end will go into the T-joint block.
8. The T-joint block, 4 by 4 by 6 inches, is hollowed out to allow the metal pipe to pass through it. The holes in the T-joint block should fit both the vertical and the bamboo feed pipes.

The best metal water pipe is copper or galvanized steel. It is also possible to use garden hose or plastic pipe.

Bamboo will split if it becomes extremely dry. In Japan, bamboo pipes are usually placed in shade or under trees, and the water keeps them moist.

Garden in an onsen town

Unzen is situated in serene and beautiful mountains in the western part of Kyushu, near Nagasaki. The area, designated as a National Park, is recognized for its spectacular seasonal splendors and for its *onsen* (hot springs). Many tourists come here from all over Japan, in all seasons, to enjoy the resort and spa. Hotels and ryokans, surrounded by their own gardens, stand on both sides of the streets. Magnificent large-scaled gardens are often to be found in hot-spring resorts such as Unzen.

A building on a hilltop slope is surrounded by shrubbery; the picture below is a near view of the house seen in the middle ground.

The long eave is supported by a number of poles. The most fascinating idea here is the use of a chain as a downspout. The chain is attached to a bamboo gutter, and leads to a pot. The draining water flows silently down the chain, into the pot, and, without splashing, overflows into the pebble-bedded drain. A close-up is on the right.

In the picture on the left-hand page, large stones border the pebbles and the lawn. From the door to the lawn, flat stones act as a walk, and serve two purposes: neatness in the design and cleanliness in the house. This is the side garden. The front garden is on the next two pages.

Though this lantern is made of four stones, each with different characteristics, its appearance is surprisingly well balanced. Only the center stone has been carved to make the shape of the light chamber. The ornamental top stone is off center, but balances with the other parts.

Stone and plants: both are important

The photographs on these two pages show interesting groupings of stones and plants. As you will notice, stones and plants are arranged harmoniously. Either stone or plant dominates; yet if one were without the other, the arrangement would be sadly lacking.

Above is a lantern backed by a boxwood shaped in clusters; juniper, azalea, stone, and *usu-ishi* (millstone) form a unit. The lantern, of course, is the chief object. We saw this type of lantern not only in the vicinity of Unzen but also in Kagoshima. Perhaps they are made of lava that flowed out here many years ago.

Above: The two rocks in this setting have a somewhat angular look, but the overall effect is softened by the surrounding plum, juniper, and azalea. This unusual display is extremely casual and unstudied.

On the left, plants and a stone are grouped; but, unlike the other two photographs, the large stone here is less noticeable because the shaped *onko* (Japanese yew) is tall, and low juniper and azalea blend in with the smooth stone.

Garden compositions

Notice the sequence of compositions in this garden; they follow one another along the wall fence. The front area is left open for a feeling of spaciousness.

The four lower photographs on these two pages show the view from the sliding windows of the house (in upper-right photograph on the next page). The map shows the positions from which the pictures were taken.

2. This view is the far left side of the garden as seen from the window area. Under the branches of the maple, a stone lantern, rock, azalea, and millstone form the composition; another one of millstone and juniper follows on the right. Notice the unusual design of the stone lantern.

3. This is the central view from the house. Here, against the fence, an old cherry tree, rocks, and azalea are grouped. Here again, at the right, juniper and stone carry the movement to the next unit. The white and dark object is a light in the garden.

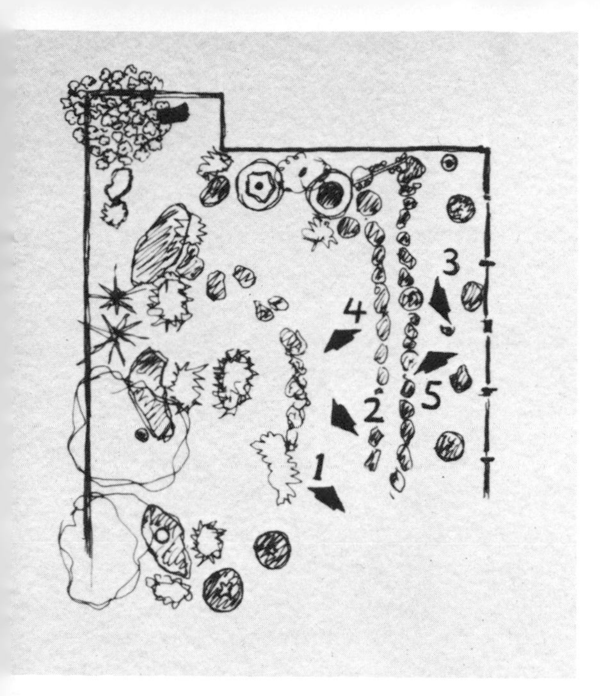

1. This is the back of the house in the photograph on page 64. The pebbles beneath the eaves are continued from the front of the house, and millstones provide an easy walkway. From these sliding windows one may see four groupings of interest in the photographs below.

4. This is the far-right view. Here, low-cut azaleas and stones make a grouping. At the rear, a pruned shrub and stone screen the corner of the wall. To the right, near the building, another stone lantern rests on an old hand mill, which in turn rests on a millstone.

5. This corner is near the window, and at the right end of the garden. While a water basin usually sits in a hollow space for drainage, here the use of a millstone is repeated at the foot of the water basin and in the accompanying stones. Notice the bamboo hishaku, or ladle, and bamboo fence.

At the lower right is the entrance gate. From the gate the paved walk turns and leads straight to the house entry, or genkan. Large stones set into the walk make an interesting pattern, and help to link the paved walk with other paths. The *machiai* (waiting booth) is at the right side of the path.

Family house: entry area

Characteristically, there is a long approach from the gate to the main entry of a Japanese home. Although it may be modest in dimensions, the entry area is of particular interest to the homeowner, and a pleasure to arriving guests.

This is the residence of Mr. and Mrs. Hisao Morita. You will see their main garden in the next pages. This long, attractive approach is flanked by a pond, which, quite large in size, is part of the main garden. As you enter the gate, your eyes are drawn to the beautiful main garden, but when you turn along the paved walk you see a cordial, intimate entrance garden with a charming waiting booth.

This is the left side of the main entrance. To the left of the paved walk, a sodegaki and tall hexagonal stone lantern, kasuga-doro, gracefully await the visitor. In front of the lantern, steppingstones lead to a wooden bridge. (See page 72.)

The right side of the entry reveals a bamboo fence and a sugi bark fence. In the foreground you can see part of the waiting booth. On the moss-covered ground between the fences and the path are an aged tree with several trunks, rock, ferns, mondo grass, and Oregon grapes.

A view from the genkan. At the end of the paved walk, to the left, is the gate. To the right, steppingstones lead to the rear of the garden.

Waiting booth, or machiai

The machiai, or waiting booth, is a small house where guests wait until the host or hostess appears for the tea ceremonial. Inside is a bench to sit on, and sometimes a room, closet, and other conveniences are provided.

In a tea garden, the machiai is required by tradition; its construction can vary from simple to elaborate. Usually, a paved walk or steppingstones lead from the waiting booth to the inside, to an inner gate, and thence to an inner garden where the tearoom stands. Quite apart from practical use, it is valued for garden ornament. The pebble-covered place is called an "eavesdrop," and the flat stone is the first steppingstone. In the foreground, to the right, steppingstones lead to a wooden bridge.

Looking outward from the zashiki. In the foreground is a low table; beyond are the engawa, a bridge, pond, and various plantings. At the left side of the bridge is the entrance area shown on the preceding page.

Wooden bridge

Because most Japanese people reflect their ideas and opinions in their gardens, each garden has its own distinctive character. Although this garden has many interesting features, elegantly arranged, its central motif is water. A large, irregular pond stretches between the entrance garden and the inner garden. The pond extends under the house floor, almost to the end of the property line (see page 75).

This bridge is made of logs laid crosswise over wooden supports. It is designed to be ornamental as well as practical.

Looking at the entry from the center of the main garden, you see that the steppingstones lead to the wooden bridge and to a paved walk. To the left is the house entry seen on the preceding pages. The bamboo-roofed edifice is the machiai; the tile roof, over main gate.

A natural source of water

There is a natural spring on this lot, and there is another pond for goldfish. At the time we visited this garden, a corner of this pond, into which the spring-water flows, was screened for young goldfish. This little pond and the large pond close by have natural clay bottoms. (No concrete was needed to hold the water.) Most Japanese waterways and ponds are lined with concrete, which is concealed by stones, pebbles, and gravel. In old ponds or streams, a clay coating was used to make the bottom impermeable; nowadays concrete is used.

One requirement of a garden is the pruning of trees and shrubs to keep them healthy and to control their sizes and shapes. Mr. Morita told us that he trims his own azaleas just after the flowers fade, breaks off the new shoots of pines in the spring to maintain a desired shape, removes old needles in the fall, and gives attention to other trees and shrubs as it is needed.

This is the right side of the garden as seen from the same zashiki shown on page 72, except that this photograph shows more of the sliding glass door beyond the engawa.

A roofed gate. Notice that the trellises and the design of the roof are a repetition of the machiai's on the last page. A bamboo fence divides the gardens. The steppingstones lead to the inner gate and then to the other part of the garden. On the left, the azalea is trimmed to the height of the large stone. Deep moss carpets the ground. In the distance you can see another kasuga-doro (lantern).

A family's main garden

The upper photograph was taken from the zashiki. On the other side of the engawa, where the glass door is open, sits a kutsunugi-ishi, or stone, and from there steppingstones lead to the left to a wooden bridge and to the right to the inner gate. A yukimi-doro, or low stone lantern, rests on a flat stone over the water as a chief ornament. A kasuga-doro (tall lantern) stands in the shadow of branches beside the gate. Mr. and Mrs. Morita's main garden, shown on this and the previous pages, contains many interesting details and elegant simplicity. From the zashiki may be seen an open area, pond, bridge, low shaped plants, gate, and fence, all blending in one harmonious whole.

In a far-right view of the garden, a tall round water basin stands near a small veranda called a *nure-en* (wet veranda) because of its exposure to the weather. The kutsunugi-ishi, the terminal steppingstone, the water basin and its accompanying stones, and the loose bamboo fence as the background, form the setting.

A close-up of the water basin and its four accompanying stones. Ordinarily, a water basin is set in a hollow of clay or concrete, but here it stands in shallow springwater that comes from the right of this area, an unusual use.

The far-left corner of the garden: Part of the large pond in the main garden reaches to the other side of this taking-off-shoes stone. Walls, sliding doors, and hanging *nokisudare* (bamboo blind) are visible. The wall facing us is the side of the genkan, or entry vestibule. The variety of plants here is interesting.

A close-up of a pond that extends under the house floor (the dark area). A supporting post rests on a natural stone pier, and little ferns grow next to the stone. Notice the two types of handrailing. The one on the left guards the sliding doors at the side, while the other rails off the little outjutting veranda.

This garden is completely enclosed: on three sides by the house and on the fourth by a high fence. One side has sliding lattice windows, but the garden is mainly to be viewed from the side of the zashiki. In the above photograph, a curved path leads to a corner at the other side of the house. The photograph at the left shows the dry pond that is the chief point of interest in this garden. The crushed stone "watercourse" from the "waterfall" in the center seems to disappear beneath the trimmed azalea.

This is the view opposite that of the picture on the preceding page. The path is a combination of steppingstones and two stretches of stones of similar size embedded in concrete.

A family garden in Tokyo

This garden is so designed that the zashiki faces the central area of garden interest. The gently curved path, which leads to the other side of the house, divides the garden diagonally, and two slightly mounded areas of uneven slope are distinctive features. In the planting area farther back to the right, a dry waterway (photograph at lower left) beginning at the foot of the planting wins attention. To the left of the path are a water basin with stones and a sodegaki; but most of this side is left open to gain a feeling of spaciousness.

This *mokkoku* (*Ternstroemia japonica*) has two main zigzag trunks. The right one is supported by two poles. The foliage is shaped into interesting clusters, with large open spaces left or created between the branches. The white smoke in the background is caused by fumes coming out of the ground in the hot-springs resort of Unzen.

The Japanese way of shaping

The Japanese gardener approaches a tree as an artist or sculptor might. His purpose is to trim and shape it into a natural work of art trained by the hand of man. He shapes a tree to harmonize with its surroundings and to emphasize the natural feeling of the garden. Most large and medium trees are shaped into graceful lines that both retain and heighten their natural form. Some low-growing trees and shrubs are trimmed into compact forms. Each plant, of course, has its own characteristic growth habit, texture, and form. One pine will grow in an airy way, with much space between its branches; another into a conical shape; maki, or yew pine, grows a little denser than pine, and in an elliptical cone shape; cypress and juniper are dense and compact.

Flowering and deciduous trees also receive pruning. They are shaped into natural forms with spacings left or created—by cutting—between the branches. In Japan some flowering plants, such as azalea, are trimmed primarily to keep their permanent compact shapes at the expense of their flowers. The purposes of pruning and trimming are mainly to control the sizes of various trees and shrubs, to keep their health, and to heighten the beauty and the dramatic presence of the plants.

This is a common shaping in Japan. A single trunk has large clusters of branches at the bottom; the clusters gradually become smaller toward the top. This wax-leaf privet was in Kyoto.

This mokkoku (*Ternstroemia japonica*) is shaped into three layers. Here, unlike the picture at the left, a group of branches and leaves form a layer. This was photographed in Unzen.

The onko (Japanese yew) can be trained into any shape. Here a low flat layer is made by many twisted branches, while three branches growing out of this layer form a sort of conical shape. This yew was in a lakeside town on Lake Toya.

This ibuki (Chinese juniper) forms a group of pompons. This species has an interesting growth habit: the leaves grow furled. The tree can also be trained into other shapes, of which you will see more in later pages.

The sizes of pines vary. Here a Japanese gardener uses a ladder to reach the top to pinch off the spring shoots.

The beginning of pine shaping

Among the most-used trees in Japan are the pines. The pines grow well anywhere in Japan; but a pine in a garden needs the hand of man if it is to play its role properly. The photographs below show newly cut-back pines. The work of cutting back on these pines at this stage looks too severe, but it is done for the best results in the future. These pines, in Kashikojima, Shima Peninsula, were photographed in May.

Shaped Japanese pines

These two pines have already been shaped. In the photograph above, branches are trained over bamboo framing. Notice that clusters are large at the lower part and become smaller toward the top. This finely shaped pine had not yet received spring attention this year.

On the right, this pine did get attention in the spring. Notice that there are no shoots on the pine. The two shapes here are quite different; though one is lush and formal, the other is spare and casual, but both are interesting.

The pine in the top picture is in Kagoshima, Kyushu; the one on the right is in Unzen. Both are in public areas.

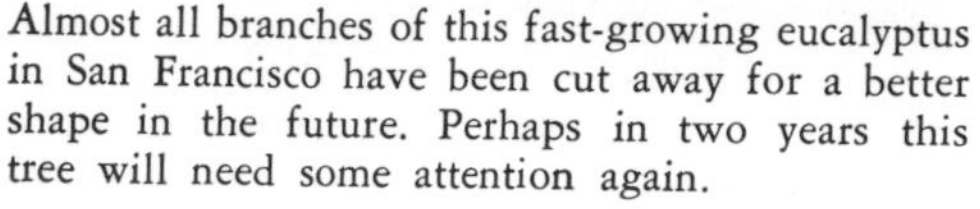

Almost all branches of this fast-growing eucalyptus in San Francisco have been cut away for a better shape in the future. Perhaps in two years this tree will need some attention again.

This pruned cherry in Kawatana was cut back because it was newly transplanted, and also for the benefit of its future shape.

Cut back to control size

We all wish to have well-shaped plants that need little care; unfortunately, there are no such plants. If you want well-shaped plants, you must work to that end. All plants are individualists, and they need your hand to restrain and guide them. The best way is to start cutting back and shaping them when they are young, like children. Often, however, we miss the first opportunity, and must do so as soon as possible thereafter. Sometimes it is necessary to cut drastically; but, if it is properly done, the plant will recover, respond, and take the desired shape in time. In general, to control size and shape, fast-growing plants naturally require more care; the slow-growing ones take less. In other words, if you want a well-shaped plant fast, then a fast-growing plant is your answer, but frequent clipping is required. With slow-growing plants, you will see results only gradually.

Cutting back a tree can be done in almost any way you wish, but it is more pleasing if the branches are thinned artistically. This tree is also in San Francisco.

The branches of this tall Himalayan cedar in Kyoto have been cut back to control size and also for the sake of appearance. It would have been easier if pruning had been started earlier.

Bamboo is also one of the most-used plants in Japanese gardens. In this view from the street, bamboo branches are pruned to make pompon shapes, a style that is often seen in Japan.

The same bamboos from the garden side. To get this shape, a Japanese gardener first cuts the bamboo branches when they are young, and then keeps repeating the process as they grow older.

Sugi in unusual shapes

The Japanese cause their plants to grow in odd shapes. Here we see gardeners taking advantage of the inherent vertical growth habit of sugi (Japanese cedar). Some branches are cut close to the trunk to bear clusters of leaves, while others are cut away to make large spaces between the pompon clusters.

Both photographs show sugi in the entrance area. Above, a shaped sugi at the side of a path screens part of the house wall.

A group of sugi, other plants, and rocks together make a circular planting area to one side of the entrance area where, again, the plants screen the side of house.

These photographs show pompons at the tops of sugi in gardens. They are quite attractive from a distance.

Right: This young shaped sugi at the side of a wall is fifteen feet tall. Notice how the branches are cut away from the trunk, while clusters of green are left. This is one of the unusual shapes that looks most dramatic at the proper place in the garden.

A large azalea is planted on an island in a pond. Here the shrub is casually trimmed to harmonize with its surroundings. This was in the garden of the Fujiya Hotel, Miyanoshita.

These azaleas are more formally trimmed to control their size, and for the next blooming. This was in Masuda.

This very large, perfectly formal shaped azalea was in Nikko. Here a group of ferns adds interest to the scene. This photograph shows that blooming time is almost over and that the azalea is ready to be trimmed for next season.

The Japanese like azaleas

The climate in Japan is just right for azaleas. They grow wild on hillsides and in the mountains and beside nursery yards. Azaleas are the most commonly used shrubs in Japanese gardens. The Japanese like them in bloom, and also admire them for their shapes and their foliage. They are trimmed into square or round forms or into ground-hugging half ovals or in complement with stonework to suggest hillocks, or they may be left natural. Again, the purpose of trimming is to keep the plants healthy and under control. The growth habit of azaleas is usually low and compact.

This short, columnar-shaped Japanese boxwood was in Heirinji Temple, west of Tokyo. To make this columnar shape interesting, clumps of mondo grass are planted at the foot of the boxwood.

An odd combination of square-shaped azalea and round-shaped privet in a corner of the Iko-zenji garden in Masuda. Notice how the aralia in the background makes the shaped plants stand out.

Compact plant shapes

The Japanese like to shape plants into compact forms that are in harmony with the planting area. Once the shape is established, seasonal trimming is necessary to maintain it. Most shrubs can be trimmed at almost any time of the year, but not azaleas. The right trimming time for azaleas is when blooming is just about finished. The Japanese use much the same tools we use for trimming—pruning shears and hedge trimmers.

This eye-catching pyramid-shaped boxwood has eight layers. One layer is about six inches thick. This was in the entrance area of the Miyako Hotel, Kyoto.

This two-layer boxwood on a slope was shaped perpendicular to the ground. Making the shape parallel to the slope is unusual. This plant was in the Iso Garden, Kagoshima.

Here a compact shaped shrub stands in front of a rock. Smooth clusters are formed on branches. This type of shaping is most popular in Japan. This plant was in Okayama.

On a hillslope, shaped azaleas surround a large stone to make a most dramatic combination. This was in the Iso Garden, Kagoshima.

All kinds of shapes

Ibuki, or Chinese juniper, is a great favorite of the plant trainer. He can make it take almost any form he desires. These two pages show its varying shapes. The juniper on the left follows its natural inclination, with the branches rolling up from the bottom like flames. The tips of the branches have not yet been cut back.

Here full-grown junipers are shaped to form a screen. Small clusters of leaves here and there show the plant's habit of furling. The dense foliage makes a very striking hedge.

These two junipers have been trimmed back to shape them and to control their size. The pruned branches form a round layer, while other branches have been cut away to create spaces between layers.

These newly transplanted large junipers are supported by posts to brace them against the wind until they take firm hold. The tips of the branches have been trimmed and the tops cut so that the junipers will remain approximately the size they are now, although they will fill out a little.

These junipers, planted in a row at the side of a driveway, are allowed to grow naturally, except that the tips of the branches are trimmed. Because the tops have not been cut away, unlike the junipers at the left, these will grow taller.

The yew pine is a Japanese favorite

The maki is another favorite plant of the Japanese gardener. This species has a growth habit and natural shape similar to those of the pines. It grows tall, and the trunk may curve. It has thick foliage, and can be shaped in clusters and in layers. In general, when Japanese gardeners shape plants, they try to follow the plants' natural growth habits. As you will have noticed, the shapes and forms given to junipers, sugi, and other plants are different from one another because the plants all grow differently.

On these two pages are shaped maki from different areas: Above, Miyazaki; right, Osaka; next page, above, Unzen; and, below, Ujiyamada. The ideas behind the shaping of all these maki are similar: Notice that the trees have spaces between the branches and that the branches are covered by layers or clusters of needles. Also, tops are clipped.

Maki are focal points in a garden

The shaped maki is usually the tallest plant in its area, and serves as one of its focal points. Of course, other plants, rocks, and ornamental objects are needed to complete the composition.

Right: These two shaped maki look somewhat like pines.

Below: The two tallest plants are shaped maki that stand out among the other trees and shrubs in this circular planting area.

This winding stream is bordered by large rocks and low-growing plants. A bridge of six-foot split logs crosses the brook. The face of the bridge consists of the split sides of the logs. The low, hewn wood railing on both sides completes the design. Small carp (*koi*) in the water add to the naturalness of the scene.

Water as the central feature of a garden

Water is often the central feature of Japanese gardens, and is employed in many ways: in waterfalls, streams, ponds, and water basins. The Japanese make an effort to emphasize water as much as possible. Its presence may be real or simply suggested. Sometimes the appearance of water in a garden is simulated by an arrangement of rocks, gravel, pebbles, plants, and other objects. A bridge may link an island to the shore, or the island may remain tranquilly isolated. A stone lantern, iron frog, tortoise, crane, or other ornament may appear on the bank. Water plants and fish often add naturalness to a pond.

Carp in the garden: color and motion

Koi are a symbol of strength. Carp leaping up a waterfall is a popular subject of Japanese art, and paper koi swimming in the wind are the symbol of Boys' Day in May in Japan. Both express the koi's liveliness.

Ponds in many Japanese gardens are colorful with flashing goldfish (*kingyo*), carp (*koi*), or trout (*masu*). As a matter of fact, some ponds are made just to display fish.

Japanese favor carp for their beautiful colors and graceful movements. These fish are strong and long-lived. Koi come in many colors—red, white, black, blue, gold—or in a combination of colors. The cost of koi varies widely, depending not only on colors and color patterns but also on the shape and balance of the body. Unlike goldfish in an aquarium, koi are looked at from above, not from the side. Temperature of water and type of soil have a great effect in the raising of koi. Cold water is better for koi's color. Though koi may grow faster in warm water, their colors may fade. Although the average life-span of koi is about seventy years, some are said to be more than two hundred years old. Such koi grow to a length of four feet. A rare koi may cost as much as $30,000, but the commoner varieties are not too expensive. Koi, like swimming jewels, can bring delightful color and motion to any garden.

Irises and casually trimmed azaleas lean over the water in this small pond. Notice the casually placed steppingstones by the side of the pond.

The pond in the lower picture is the same area that is shown on the jacket of this book. The elaborate yukimi-doro is a heavier accent among the delicate lines of plants along the edge of the pond. Colorful koi bring natural motion to this tranquil setting.

The path leads to steps where shaped azaleas and stone are placed to denote the beginning of the rise. At the right of the steps are pine and azalea for screening.

By the side of the pond

Banks are not simply the dividing line between land and water. They have a direct and important effect on the beauty of the pond or stream, and therefore on the total composition of the garden. This is a corner of a garden at the Chorakuen Hotel in Tamatsukuri. At the left are a distant view and, below, a close-up.

At the edge of the water, what appears to be cut logs of uneven height are driven into the bank as piling. (Actually, they are concrete posts made in the likeness of wood.) A variety of stones and concrete posts defines the flower bed of iris. Although flowering plants are not much used in Japanese gardens, irises are favored near water, and contribute great charm to the bankside.

In this beautiful pond, a stone island is combined with a light fountain. Notice the interesting shoreline: stones leaning over the water, shrubs, a drooping branch, ripples on the surface.

A rock island in a pond

One characteristic of a traditional Japanese garden is a pond with an island in it. Depending on the size of the pond, the island may bear earth, stones, and plants on it or may simply be symbolized by a single stone or group of stones. Usually, plants are placed on the shore so that they lean over, or branches of trees are allowed to droop toward the surface. In addition, there is an overflow outlet that may or may not be noticeable.

The shoreline of this pond is composed of stones and shrubs, and the pond has a rock island in the center. At the lower left, between a group of stones, is the overflow outlet where the water slides quietly over rocks. This pond is in Miyanoshita.

A stream bed of crushed stones fills the flat area of the dry pond, which is bordered with large stones. The large upright stone at the upper left represents a hill, while the group of steplike stones beside it suggests a waterfall. This was in Shimabara, Kyushu.

Water is important even when it's missing

Water is often suggested by an arrangement of rocks, stones, gravel, pebbles, sand, plants, and ornamental objects. If a true pond or creek has no water in it, it is still a dry pond or creek. But in Japan a dry pond or stream is purposely designed with water in a symbolic form.

In constructing such a pond or stream, bordering materials are carefully selected and placed to suggest a pond or stream in nature. Gravel, sand, pebbles, or crushed stones fill the dry waterway. Here, on two pages, we show examples of simulated watercourses.

The suggestion of water

The photograph at the upper right was taken from the second floor of a house. Although there is no water, the arrangement of stones, natural soil, and trimmed plants gives the impression of a pond. Notice that the placement of stones in the center of the picture indicates a waterfall. This is in Nikko.

Below: This small corner grouping of large, medium, and small rocks in the midst of sand represents an island in an ocean. This was in Suizenji Park, Kumamoto.

These two ways of suggesting water without actually using it are characteristic of Japanese garden design. The Japanese feel that such compositions have inner beauty, and it is up to the viewer to be able to appreciate it.

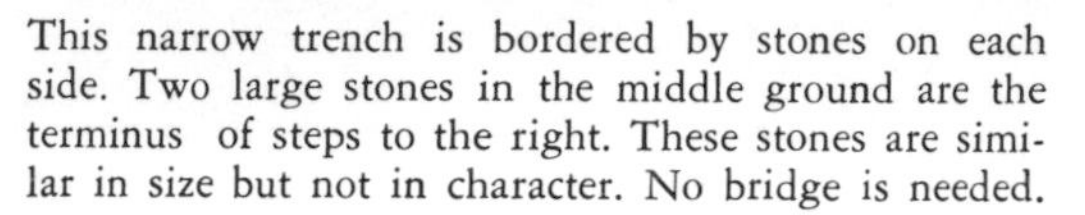

This narrow trench is bordered by stones on each side. Two large stones in the middle ground are the terminus of steps to the right. These stones are similar in size but not in character. No bridge is needed.

Here a single slab spans the trench. The near side of the path is covered with fine gravel; and the other side, with large crushed stones for contrast. The arrangement is an ingenious way of integrating textures.

Crossing over water

If a waterway in the garden is to be crossed, some passage is needed—stepping-stones or a bridge. A garden bridge made of stone, natural or worked wood, or of other materials is often more decorative than practical. In other words it is not, sometimes, easy to walk on. In these two pages we show some interesting ideas for crossing a waterway.

In this narrow stream three millstones are placed in the water for easy passage. However, steppingstones laid in the same manner are more common.

The ends of four cut granite slabs lie next to one another over an iris pond. The bridge is not easy to cross, but it is very decorative, and contrasts handsomely with the surrounding plants.

A zigzag hewn stone bridge spans part of a rather large pond. The ends of each granite slab meet side by side, and the joints are supported by granite posts, forming a most attractive ornamental bridge. The zigzag plan is characteristic of Japanese design.

Let's call it "bam-boom"

Sozu is the Japanese name for the device you see on these pages. There is no word for *sozu* in English. Some people call it a "waterwheel," but of course it is not really a wheel. We have invented our own name for it—"bam-boom"—because it is made of bamboo, tilts to empty itself, and in doing so makes a sound.

Sozu in the pond

The sozu (bam-boom), which are often seen in Japanese gardens, are accessories. Though they differ one from another, their basic principle is always the same. The sozu on these pages is placed in a corner of a pond. Because the garden is a broad one, it is not easy to see the sozu, but everyone in the garden hears its sound. Near the right leg of the yukimidoro, which may be seen on the other side of the bridge, is a bamboo flume tied to the trunk of a pine, while a bamboo pipe receives water from the flume. This arrangement is the sozu.

Sounds in a Japanese garden

Many years ago, the sozu was used along a mountain stream to scare off, with its sound, a wild boar that came to ravage the vegetation. As with some other garden ornaments, though it has lost its original use, it has become a favorite garden accessory. The intermittent sound of the bamboo pipe hitting its stone resting place can be very pleasing.

Bringing sound into gardens is not a recent idea among the Japanese. The plashing of a waterfall, the dripping of water from a bamboo flume into a water basin, the sibilant rustling of a stream, the light chiming of a wind-bell—all these sounds have long been heard in Japanese gardens.

In this water garden, the sozu is placed in harmony with several other ornaments: the large yukimi-doro on a big rock, stone frogs, surrounding rocks and plants.

The photograph at the left shows water dripping from a bamboo flume into the diagonally cut end of the sozu. When enough has been collected, the diagonal end drops, and the water flows out (above); then the other end of the sozu returns to its former position, hitting a rock at the base (in this garden both water and rock), making a hollow sound. The intervals between sounds depend, of course, on how long it takes for water to fill the rocking cup.

Bam-boom in a stream

This sozu in a stream is simply made. The bases of the vertical supports are buried in the stream bed, and rocks are placed on top of the bases to secure them. The feed pipe, which carries water into the cup of the rocking pipe, is an ordinary steel pipe hidden under a rock. Notice that part of the water falls into the pipe but also that some does not. Such "loss" of part of the water is purposely sought in design because too much water feeding into the pipe would result in a busy up-and-down motion, and any sound too frequently heard will be bothersome rather than pleasant. Notice, also, that the end of the rocking pipe touches the stone at just the right angle.

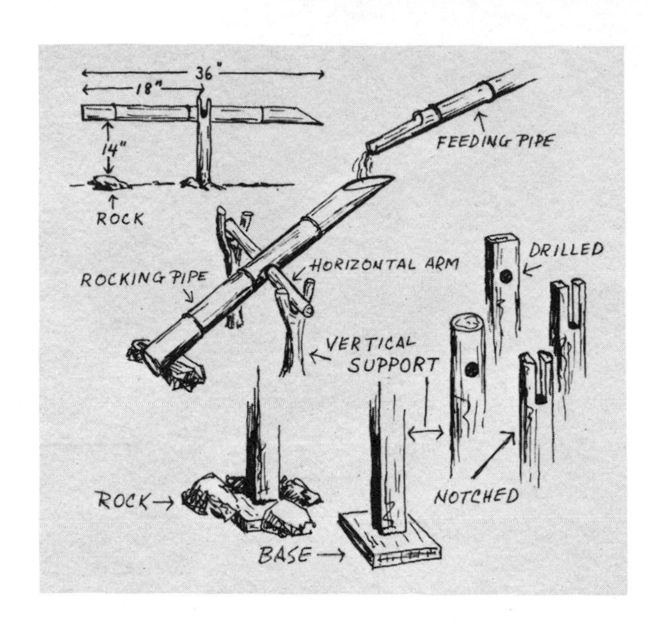

How to make a sozu

A sozu is made with a few pieces of bamboo and wooden materials. The illustration above shows its details.

The central drawing shows a complete sozu. The principle of the seesaw is applied. As water enters into the cup of the rocking pipe, the weight of the water makes the cup decline gradually; finally, the diagonal end tips to empty the collected water. After the water has flowed out, the diagonal side, being lighter, rises, and the other, heavy, end lowers to strike a stone at the base and make a sound.

The rocking pipe and the horizontal arm must be secured. One end of the bamboo rocking pipe is cut diagonally, and that side is placed upward to receive water from the bamboo flume or feed pipe. The bamboo rocking pipe is about 36 inches in length and 2 to 3 inches in diameter. The height between the rocking pipe and waterline is about 14 inches. The horizontal arm thrusts about the center of the bamboo rocking pipe, and this joint should be tight.

Two supporting poles may be stakes, twigs, log, or even 2-by-4-inch lumber. Support should be loose to permit movement of the horizontal arm.

The bases of the supporting poles should be stable. Use stones or set the poles in concrete. See page 63 to find out how the bamboo water feed pipe is made.

A surprising waterfall

It is exciting to watch and to listen to this magnificent waterfall. This dramatic man-made fall is about 100 feet in length and 8 feet high. The amount of falling water is controlled by the amount of water in a small reservoir, which looks somewhat like a pond, located above the fall. Naturally, the sound varies with the volume of falling water.

Trees and shrubs planted behind the stream that feeds the fall give depth to the scene, and creates the illusion of a forest. In this setting, the width and abrupt plunge of the fall come as a surprise. The fall has a winding edge over which the water cascades in uneven segments. Large rocks enhance the lower pond, into which the fall empties, and the otherwise flat foreground. The lawn area ends in a gracefully curved shoreline.

This beautiful waterfall is in the garden of the Sapporo Park Hotel in Hokkaido.

Panoramic view of a large waterfall

This is the waterfall seen on the preceding pages, but viewed, this time, from above. This photograph helps to explain how such a dramatic effect can be achieved in a relatively compact garden area. The light area at the top is the street. Next is a planting area with shrubs and trees, some supported by poles because the garden is new. There is a water basin, and the cherry trees are in bloom (the light-colored trees). A reservoir winds along above the fall. Large rocks are scattered in the pond. Small stones form the pond bed and line the shore. The curved shoreline complements the winding edge of the fall. Steppingstones pass through the pond area to unite water and lawn. Though the planting area above is quite narrow, the fall is not visible from the street; and from the level of the lawn in the garden, the street is completely excluded.

A natural waterfall in the woods of Hakone reminded us of the man-made fall we had seen in Sapporo. Here spring water cascades down the face of a ragged cliff while protruding rocks make the water splash and separate into hundreds of individual small cataracts.

What makes a waterfall splash

This is a close-up of part of the Sapporo waterfall pictured on page 106. The volume of falling water is much less in this photograph. Some water falls straight down, while some strikes the ledges and joints of the wall, and splashes outward. Slower-dripping water along the stone cracks behind the veil of water forms interesting white lines.

Wall of waterfall without water

This picture shows how a waterfall wall looks without water. Noticc how quiet and restful the scene is without the lively motion of water. The top edge is irregular to make the flow of water uneven. The irregular cracks between the great stones also affect the flow of the fall, as does the volume of water allowed to come over. The ideas worked out so very well in this waterfall are quite applicable to a home garden on a smaller scale, with a simple recirculating pump so that the water may be used again and again.

Making a waterfall

A waterfall is a great device for simulating nature in the garden. It can be represented so naturally that you might almost think you came upon it in a recess of the mountains. People who like gardens, and who are prepared to construct a waterfall of their own, often want more than just a simple descent of water from a higher level to a lower one. It is quite possible to have the water descend from a cliff formed by rocks. The lower part of the cliff is the outlet of the fall; and, usually, it is a good idea to have some recessed space behind the outlet to form a reservoir for the fall. It may be elevated ground with dense planting or a stream dammed farther back to achieve a sense of depth.

A tree or trees can be planted to veil the outlet of the waterfall, which can be surrounded with thick foliage and various groups of stones to suggest a splendid mountain setting. The edge and height of the cliff will determine the shape and character of your fall. It can be wide or narrow, high or low, straight or wavy, two-sided, lacy, a single drop, or one broken by rocky steps.

Naturally, the volume of water determines the character of its movement and the impact of water on the rocks at the bottom that creates its sound. If the waterfall forms a stream that is the source of a pond, the stream will be narrow at its origin, gradually becoming wider as it nears the pond. The stream should curve, and vary its width before it empties into the pond. Plants and stones should border the banks of a stream, and very often stones are placed in midstream to break the even or otherwise monotonous flow of the water. Sometimes a stream cascades as swiftly as a mountain torrent; at others, it moves leisurely.

This is a two-stepped waterfall. The lower fall is four feet high. Note that both falls have rock backgrounds with plants placed to create depth and to give a natural effect. Here the water drops to a fall basin wherein it splashes, separates, and gathers again into a stream. The next page shows where it goes. This garden is in Nakajima Park, Sapporo, Hokkaido.

The waterfall on the preceding page flows into this stream. The banks of the stream, formed of unevenly placed rough stones, give a rugged, mountainous feeling. The churning cascade makes a rushing sound.

This is the reverse view of the picture at the left. The stones placed horizontally at the lip of the small fall dam the water, creating a small pond. Sharp, zigzag edges guide the water into different cascades.

Water from the stream, above, empties into this small, quiet lake. Its entry is near the dark tree at the left. Cherry trees are in bloom in the distance. The water serves as a mirror, reflecting trees, cherry blossoms, and a tall stone lantern.

Another view of the lake. One of the islands bears trees, shrubs, and a handsome low stone lantern. Man-made Japanese lakes often contain islands as reminders of the natural scene all about them—islands amid the ocean.

Two other islands in the same lake. A curved granite bridge connects the large and small islands. Another lantern stands on a stone base in the water. The flat stone in the foreground may be reached from the shore. The islands in this lake are designed so that, regardless of your vantage point, you may always see them.

Here water comes from underneath the rock and flows down the pebble-bedded stream. Actually, this is a spring.

Where the water comes from

In constructing a waterfall or a stream, most Japanese garden designers try to have the water come from a hidden source. Stones and plants are most commonly used to camouflage the exact starting point. The water simply appears from behind a rock or between rocks and plants.

This tall waterfall is not only pleasing to look at, but the sound of its water splashing into the small pond is also delightful to hear. Plants overhanging both sides of the fall sometimes extend beyond the height of the fall, thereby contributing to the naturally vertical composition. In this arrangement the source of the water is not visible because of dense foliage.

The natural setting for this waterfall is created by a still pond and dense plantings. Details include an island, a stone lantern, and two steppingstones. The fall is recessed, and branches veil its outlet.

The volume of the water and the rock formations at the mouth and at the bottom create the descent, splash, and sound of the fall. Because the edge of the fall protrudes, the little dam at the top of the waterfall is visible.

This stream originates somewhere in the undergrowth, and flows down into the pond. The first drop is about eight inches, with the water falling upon stones embedded in the pond.

Though this is a small waterfall, it is one of the highlights of this pond. To the right of the juniper, near the rock, is the spring that is the source of water.

A small waterfall at a Japanese inn

Ponds may come in many different sizes and shapes. A man-made pond may be round, oval, square, half-moon, or have some intricate curved shape. Most often, it will appear to be quite natural, but is artfully designed with rocks and plants. The border is usually irregular, and so arranged as not to reveal its exact contour. To add interest, and provide a source of water, a waterfall or a stream flows into the pond. An artificial hill, plants, stones, and ornamental objects are all employed to make the area around the pond more interesting.

The bottom of the pond is often covered by stones, pebbles, or gravel to conceal the artificial concrete surface. Sometimes a large stone is placed off center in the pond to suggest an island. Floating water plants and koi or other fish add color.

Here you see a pond and small waterfall laid out in natural and pleasing manner in Hokkaido, but similar ponds and waterfalls can be found almost anywhere in Japan.

The beauty of this garden is the rock arrangement on the hillside and the rocks in the water. At the left above, where you see a group of stones, is the waterfall (see preceding page). Notice the irregular shoreline of the pond and the different sizes of the rocks. The stones in the water add interest. Plants, among them birch and Japanese yew, are arranged with studied casualness.

At the edge of a more formal, paved terrace, a line of irregular rock slabs creates an informal shoreline. On the far bank, in contrast, piled-up stones and plants slope upward.

A garden pond near Lake Toya

Lake Toya, a caldera lake, on Japan's northernmost island of Hokkaido, is known for its atmosphere of calm beauty. A thickly wooded island, Nakanoshima, stands in the middle of the lake, and on sunny days Mount Yotei, famous for its graceful contour, can be seen in the background from the town of Toyako Spa. The climate is generally cool because of its northerly location, and much of the fauna and flora are unique to Hokkaido. Birch and local species of conifer grow thickly in the woods surrounding Lake Toya.

The photographs on these two and the previous two pages were made at the lakeside of the Hotel Manseikaku. The area of the pond and hill is about 15 by 30 feet.

This view looks toward the lake, and shows one side of the pond. The bank is strengthened by stones. A rock in the water suggests an island. The calm water in the pond mirrors the beautiful reflection of lovely rhododendrons and Japanese yew. Through the open fence, Lake Toya and Nakanoshima, the central island, may be seen.

Because this garden is near a river, water is drawn into the stream directly from the river. The stone stairs lead onto a curved stone bridge. Two large rocks and a trimmed azalea over them form a pleasant area on the bank of the stream.

This stream seen in the upper photograph winds to reach, finally, this little fall. The water splashes down from one flat stone to another, and then slips into the pond. At the left are neatly trimmed azaleas, and on the right, iris, a most attractive setting for an outlet.

Water garden in Kagoshima

Kagoshima, one of the largest cities on Kyushu, is located at the southern tip of Japan. Many tourists come here the year around, drawn by the long history of the city as a castle town, and by the prospect of a trip across Kagoshima Bay to the active volcano Sakurajima. Sakurajima, until fifty years ago an island, became a peninsula when the flow of lava choked up the narrow channel. Huge white radishes, often over twenty inches in diameter and weighing more than fifty pounds, grow on Sakurajima.

Iso Park, in the city, is another place well worth seeing. A villa and a traditional Japanese garden, rich in natural beauty, are in the park.

This is a different part of the pond shown on the previous page. This type of stone lantern is called a *kotoji;* it is quite ornamental. A curved stone bridge springs across the water. Both mondo grass, in the foreground, and cycad palms, behind the bridge, grow well in this southern region.

In this part of Japan, azaleas are trimmed into most attractive shapes. On the right, wisteria is trained on a trellis over the water. These are very beautiful in the spring, when in bloom. This type of garden landscape can be found in many places in Japan.

A simple yet charming hewn granite lantern in a bamboo grove. Ferns in front add interest.

Bamboo and pond garden in Kyoto

This thick, giant bamboo garden is behind a pond. Here the path, lantern, stream, and bridge create a dramatic scene. The banks of the pond are built of large and small rocks of varying shapes, and tufts of mondo grass curve over in an interesting way. Overhanging pine branches are supported by cedar poles that, as part of the garden design, are inconspicuous. The stone lantern in the lower picture is here concealed behind the hanging pine branch.

The side of a house and a kutsunugi-ishi, from which a pathway leads to the bridge. The dark stone in the rear of the bridge is the water basin you see below.

A square-shaped water basin is usually an enclosure for a well or spring. This spring is one of the sources of the pond-garden, and it overflows to the pebbles below.

This view is the right side of the garden on the preceding page, and shows the stream passing underneath the curved bridge and flowing into the small pond. The stream divides the bamboo groves. The posts of the house rest on a stone foundation. Carefully selected stones create the gentle slope of the shore. New bamboos will shoot out in the spring, after which either old or new ones, whichever seem out of keeping with the garden design, will be removed.

A view from the engawa, which is on the left. Here the garden lies between two separate wings of the house. The winding stream divides the garden area in two.